What's Your Story, Ana?

by Jennie Cole

Gate HOUSE

What's Your Story, Ana?
Copyright © Jennie Cole 2020

Published in 2020 by Gatehouse Media Limited

ISBN: 978-1-84231-198-1

British Library Cataloguing-in-Publication Data:
A catalogue record for this book is available from the British Library

No part of this publication may be reproduced in any form or by any means, electronic, mechanical, photocopying, recording or otherwise, without the prior written consent of the publishers.

This series is inspired by my students,
who all have a story to tell.

Special thanks to Ana.

Ana

My name is Ana. I come from the Republic of Moldova and my language is Romanian.

Moldova is a landlocked country in Eastern Europe. There is Romania to the west and Ukraine to the north, east and south.

When I first came to the UK, I worked on a farm. Now I live in Leeds, which is in the North of England.

I am 35 years old and I have a family who live with me in Leeds.

There are lots of cafés, restaurants and shops in the city centre and, at the weekend, it can get very busy.

I try to go into the city centre on a weekday when it's not as crowded.

I usually get the bus into the city centre from my house.

The buses are regular and it only takes about twenty minutes to get there.

There are plenty of shops to choose from.

I like the big shopping centres the best, as everything is under one roof.

When everything is under one roof, it makes shopping easier.

I enjoy looking around the shops by myself when I have the time. It's difficult to go around the shops with young children.

I have a young son and daughter and I enjoy looking in the shop windows to get ideas of what to buy them.

I can plan ahead and, if I see something, I can go back to the shop when they have a good sale.

I love browsing around the shop floors and clothes rails. I don't plan on buying, but I enjoy looking.

I check for half price and two for one offers, as this can save a lot of money, if it's something that I need anyway.

Sometimes I go into the changing rooms just to try things on.

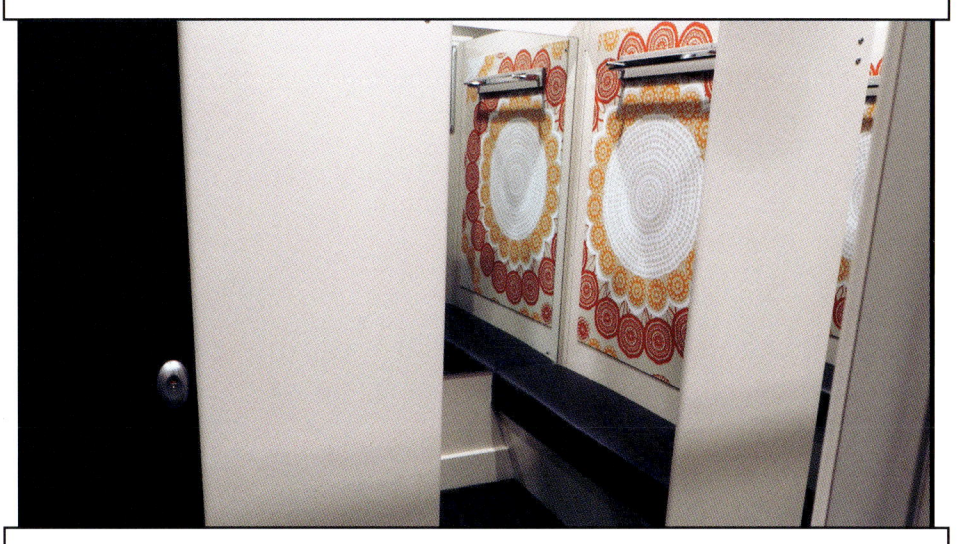

There's usually a rail in the changing rooms for me to hang up the clothes.

Sometimes I choose clothes that I would normally wear and might buy in the future.

Sometimes I try things that I wouldn't normally wear, but they are fun to try on in the changing rooms!

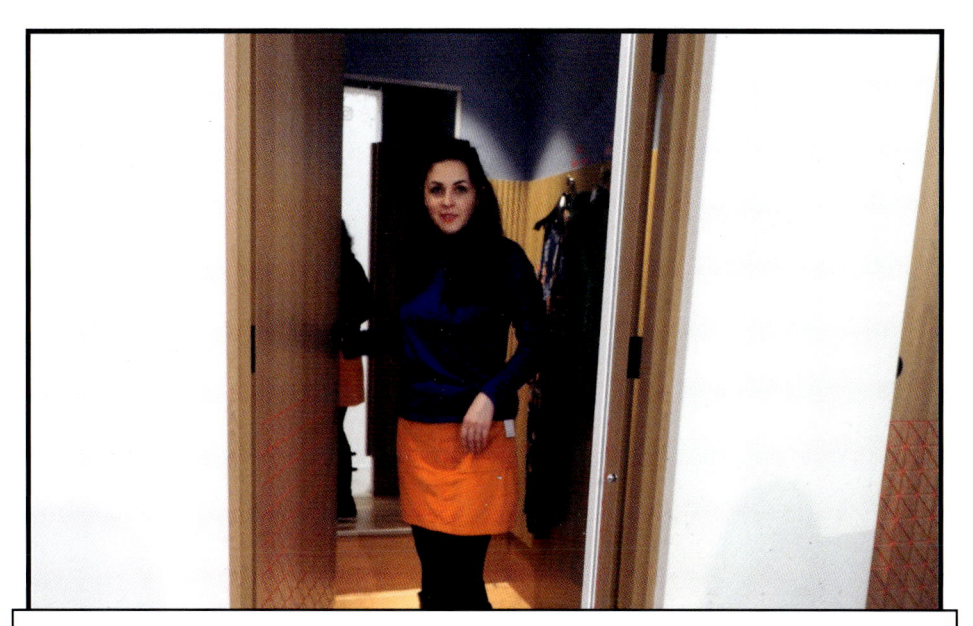

It's fun and is a bit of time out for myself.

If I see something I like, I buy it, but most of the time I can wait until the sales.

The changing rooms always have big mirrors, so it's easy to see how something looks.

The mirrors are useful if I don't go with a friend who can give me some advice.

I like trying on dresses the best.

This one has a floral pattern. I like the yellow colour too. It's a very happy colour!

Some of the shops have evening dresses that I like trying on.

Maybe I will come back and buy this black dress if I get an invitation to a party.

I like blouses that have bright, bold patterns like this one.

I like the purple and gold colours, as well as the blue stripes.

The blouse would go with a lot of other things that I have already got in my wardrobe.

I find jeans very comfortable to wear and there are lots to choose from in the city centre shops.

The hardest item to find is a warm coat that I can wear in the autumn and winter months.

There are lots of different styles to choose from.

There are coats for every occasion.

This tartan pattern looks smart for everyday wear.

I like coats with pockets to put my keys and purse in and, if it's cold, I can keep my hands warm.

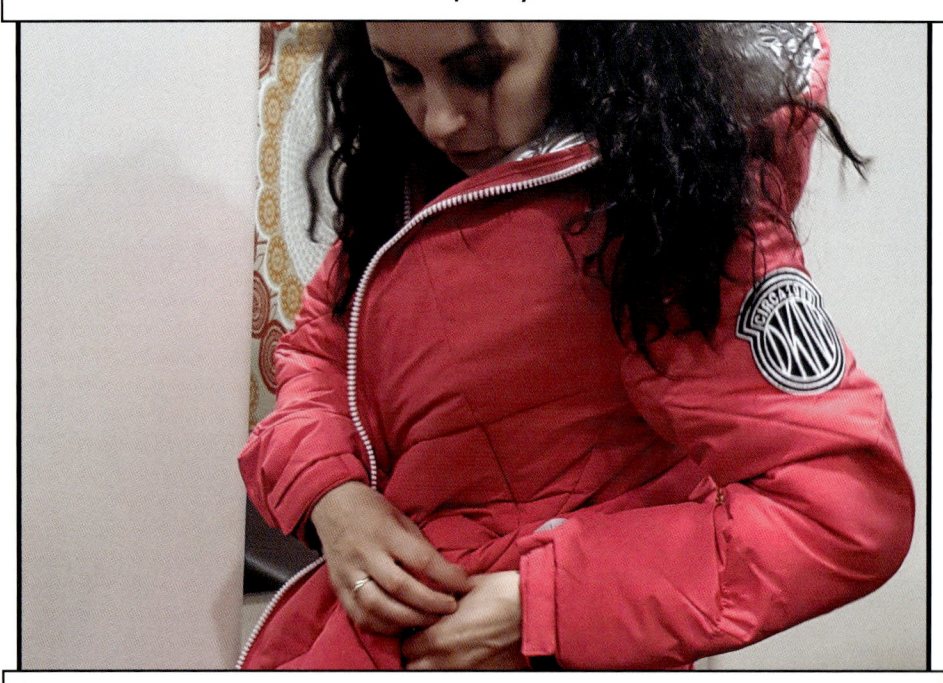

A coat with a hood is useful, if it starts to rain and I haven't got an umbrella with me.

I like to try on boots in the shops. Ankle boots are my favourite kind of boots.

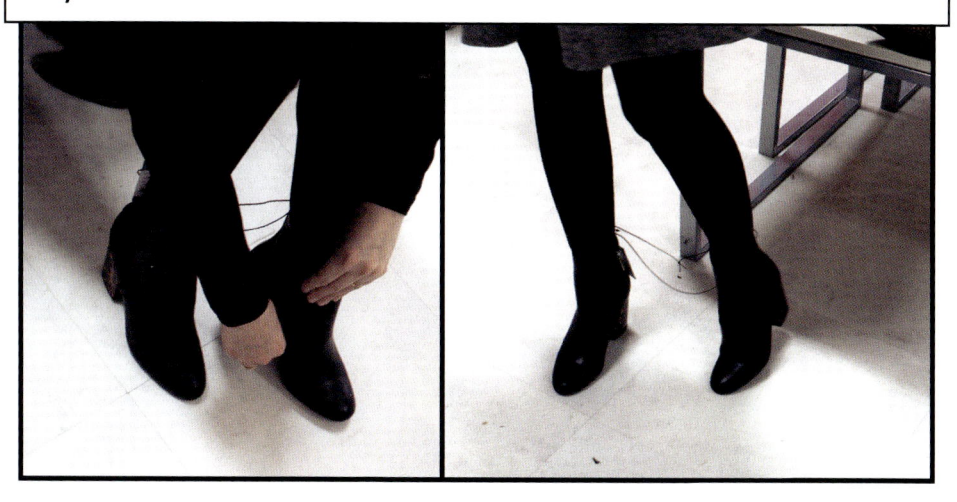

At the start of the autumn season, the shops have a good selection to choose from.

After a busy day window shopping and trying on clothes, I like to go home to my family.

Family means everything to me.

When we meet someone and ask "Where are you from?" or "What do you enjoy doing?" what we are really asking is "What's your story?"

When we start to share our story with others, we can begin to celebrate differences and recognise how much we all have in common.

Gatehouse Books®

Gatehouse Books are written for older teenagers and adults who are developing their basic reading and writing or English language skills.

The format of our books is clear and uncluttered. The language is familiar and the text is often line-broken, so that each line ends at a natural pause.

Gatehouse Books are widely used within Adult Basic Education throughout the English speaking world. They are also a valuable resource within the Prison Education Service and Probation Services, Social Services and secondary schools - both in basic skills and ESOL teaching.

Catalogue available

Gatehouse Media Limited
PO Box 965
Warrington
WA4 9DE

Tel: 01925 267778
E-mail: info@gatehousebooks.com
Website: www.gatehousebooks.com